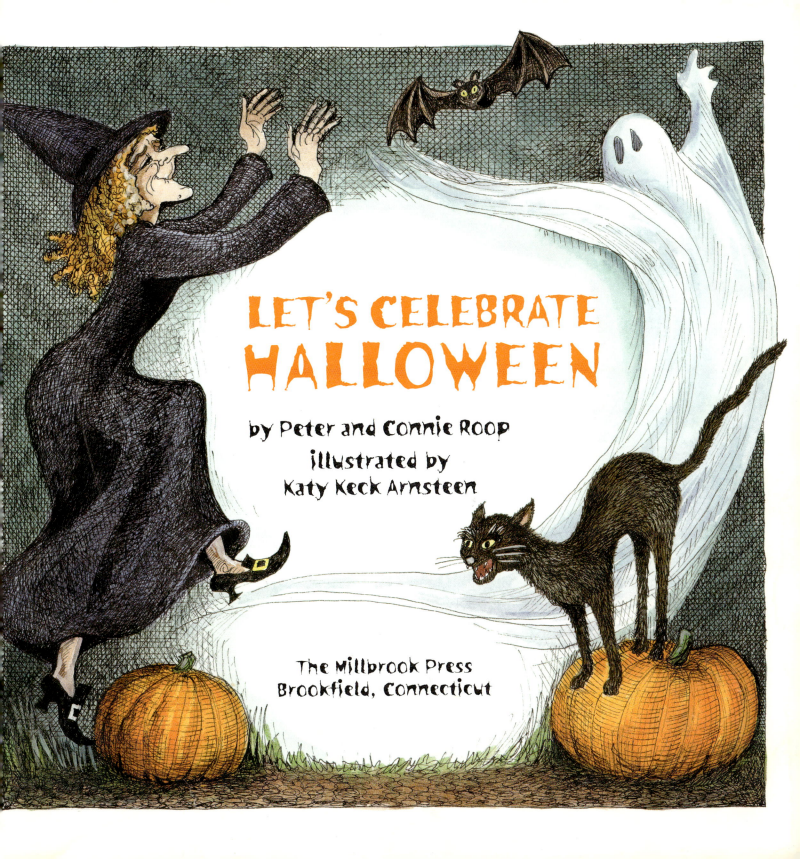

LET'S CELEBRATE HALLOWEEN

by Peter and Connie Roop

illustrated by
Katy Keck Arnsteen

The Millbrook Press
Brookfield, Connecticut

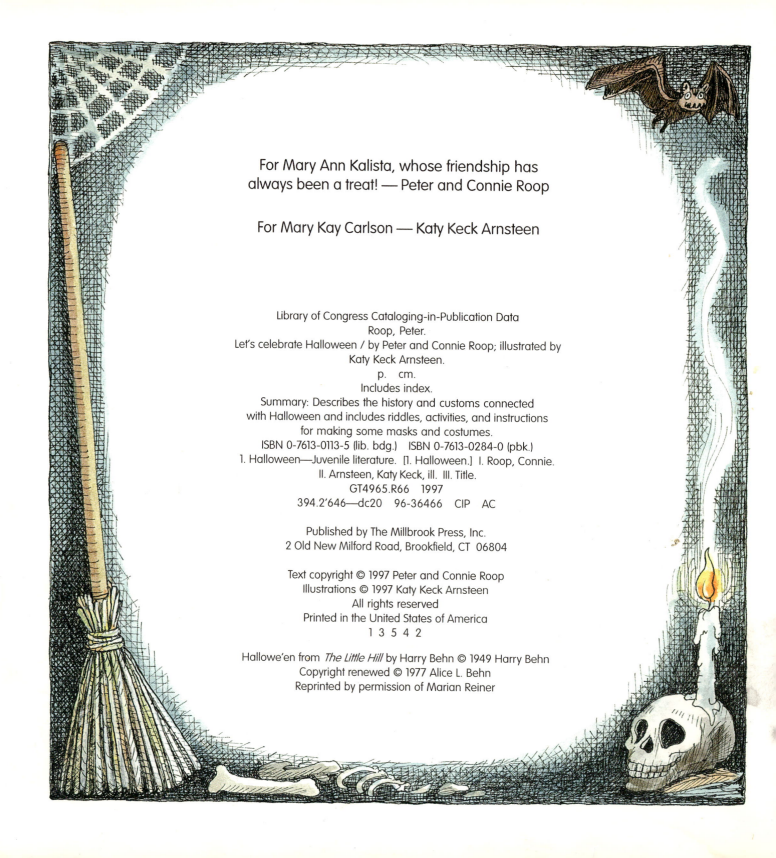

For Mary Ann Kalista, whose friendship has always been a treat! — Peter and Connie Roop

For Mary Kay Carlson — Katy Keck Arnsteen

Library of Congress Cataloging-in-Publication Data
Roop, Peter.
Let's celebrate Halloween / by Peter and Connie Roop; illustrated by Katy Keck Arnsteen.
p. cm.
Includes index.
Summary: Describes the history and customs connected with Halloween and includes riddles, activities, and instructions for making some masks and costumes.
ISBN 0-7613-0113-5 (lib. bdg.)   ISBN 0-7613-0284-0 (pbk.)
1. Halloween—Juvenile literature. [1. Halloween.] I. Roop, Connie.
II. Arnsteen, Katy Keck, ill. III. Title.
GT4965.R66   1997
394.2'646—dc20   96-36466   CIP   AC

Published by The Millbrook Press, Inc.
2 Old New Milford Road, Brookfield, CT 06804

Hallowe'en from *The Little Hill* by Harry Behn © 1949 Harry Behn
Copyright renewed © 1977 Alice L. Behn
Reprinted by permission of Marian Reiner

The doorbell rings. You open the door.
You see witches, ghosts, goblins, and vampires!
They shout, "Trick or Treat!" What night is it?
Halloween!

HOW DID HALLOWEEN BEGIN?

Long ago, people believed that evil spirits stole the sun at the end of summer. These spirits hid the sun during winter, making the days short and the nights long. People dreaded this dark and dreary time of year. The worst night of all was October 31.

The Celts, in Britain and France, held a festival called Samhain (sow-whin) on October 31. During Samhain devils, witches, and goblins roamed the countryside stealing animals, overturning carts, and playing tricks. The Celts burned bonfires to frighten away these terrible spirits. People also wore costumes of animal skins and heads to hide themselves.

In later years Samhain was combined with the Roman festival Faralia, which honored and welcomed the spirits. Then Christians began to celebrate All Saints' Day on November 1. They did this to make people stop celebrating Samhain. The evening before November 1 was called Hallow or Holy Evening. Over the years, it changed to Hallows Evening, then Hallow E'en, and now Halloween.

Many Japanese honor their ancestors during Bon, the Festival of the Dead. This celebration is held on July 13.

In India, camel bones are buried under the door to keep ghosts out.

The Hopi Indians hold a festival for their dead in June, on the longest day of the year. This is when they believe the sun is as high as it can go.

In Germany, a nightmare is called a "goblin squeeze."

Halloween was also called Nutcrack Night or Snap Apple Night in England.

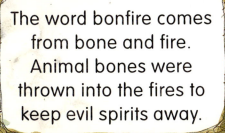

The word bonfire comes from bone and fire. Animal bones were thrown into the fires to keep evil spirits away.

In Mexico, toys are put out for children who have died, and bakers sell "Dead Men's Bread" shaped like skulls.

In France on Halloween, children ask for flowers to put on graves in cemeteries.

WHY DO GHOSTS HAUNT ON HALLOWEEN?

The word ghost sends shivers up some folks' spines. Today we think of ghosts as pale, moaning, unhappy spirits haunting on Halloween night. But this has not always been so.

Many years ago some people believed ghosts were the spirits of their dead relatives who came home to visit once a year, on Halloween. Huge fires were kept burning on hilltops to guide these friendly ghosts home. The ghosts were welcomed with feasts of nuts, apples, cakes, bread, and meat.

But people thought if the ghosts did not get enough treats, they would become angry. They would then play terrible tricks, like stealing children or killing cows and horses.

A ghost who haunts by making noises or moving objects is known as a poltergeist (pole-ter-guyst). They move chairs and beds. They rattle dishes or make pictures fall off walls. Poltergeists haunt any time they want, not only on Halloween.

Ghosts don't have shadows and leave no footprints.

If you hang a mirror on your door, ghosts will stay away.

If a candle flame turns blue, it means a ghost is in the house.

If you throw a key at a ghost, the ghost will disappear.

To keep ghosts away, you should wear red or carry a bright light.

If you turn your pockets inside out, ghosts will be scared of you!

Q. What does a ghost write with?
A. Invisible ink.

Q. What is a ghost's favorite painting?
A. The Moan-a Lisa.

Q. What kinds of keys do ghosts use?
A. Spook-keys and skeleton keys.

Q. What do ghosts fly in?
A. Scare-planes.

WHY DO WE CARVE PUMPKINS ON HALLOWEEN?

Long ago, children in Ireland made lanterns from large turnips. They hollowed out the turnips and carved faces in them. Candles inside the turnips were lit to make scary faces to frighten away evil spirits.

When the Irish came to America, they found pumpkins growing here. Since pumpkins ripen around the middle of October they became part of the Halloween tradition. Today we call carved pumpkins Jack-o'-Lanterns. Here is one version of the story that explains why.

Once upon a time there was an Irishman named Jack. Jack loved to play tricks on the Devil. Once he tricked the Devil into changing himself into a coin. Jack put the Devil into his pocket and wouldn't let him out until he promised to leave Jack alone. Another time Jack tricked the Devil into climbing a tree to get him an apple. When the Devil was in the tree, Jack carved a cross on the trunk. Because the Devil was scared of the cross, he stayed in the tree until Jack let him down.

The Devil got angry at Jack for playing so many tricks. One night he waited for Jack to walk by. He tossed a glowing coal into Jack's lantern. Because it was the Devil's coal, Jack could not blow it out.

"Jack," the Devil said, "your punishment for tricking me is to walk the Earth forever carrying your lantern lighted with my coal. People everywhere will call you Jack of the Lantern."

In Africa pumpkins were said to grow where a devil died.

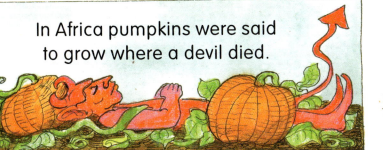

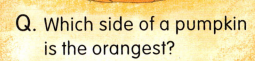

Q. Which side of a pumpkin is the orangest?

A. The outside.

Pumpkins were once used for cutting hair. A pumpkin shell was placed upside down on a boy's head. His hair was then trimmed.

The largest pumpkin grown so far weighed 990 pounds!

Other names for Jack-o'-Lanterns:

HOB-O-LANTERNS
PUNKIES
BOGIES

Q. Who is Jack-o'-Lantern's best friend?

A. Jill-o'-Lantern.

In Sycamore, Illinois, over five tons of pumpkins are carved during a Halloween Pumpkin Festival.

WHY DO WE HAVE WITCHES ON HALLOWEEN?

Imagine a witch riding her broom with a black cat perched behind her. Her nose is long and pointed. She wears a tall hat, a black dress, and a cape.

There were witches long before there ever was a Halloween. The word witch used to mean "the wise one." People would come to witches for medicines, to hear their fortunes told, or to get magic charms. Witches also provided poisons for people who wished to harm their enemies.

Witches met in small groups called covens. Each coven had thirteen people: twelve members and a leader. Covens met to practice magic, compare remedies and potions, and socialize. Even today thousands of men, women, and children who believe in witchcraft meet in covens.

People used to believe that there were three kinds of magic. The first kind was harmless white magic. A farmer might mutter a spell to make good weather come. Or a girl might use a charm to get a husband.

The second kind was black magic. The witches who practiced black magic were said to work with the Devil. They cast spells to cause sickness or death. They could cause floods, fires, and other disasters.

The worst kind of magic was performed by witches who had sold their souls to the Devil. If a witch had a wart or a mole on her body it was a sign that the Devil had bitten her. Now she belonged to the Devil. If these witches were discovered, they were burned or hanged.

Twice a year witches from one region or country would gather for special celebrations called Witches' Sabbaths. One festival was held in the spring. The other was held at Halloween.

These festivals were happy times with dancing, marriage ceremonies, and feasting. Witches played music on their Devil's bagpipes, made from cats' tails and hens' heads. Thousands of people came to these celebrations, whether they were witches or not.

People accused of being witches were sometimes thrown into ponds with their hands tied to their feet. If they floated, it meant they were real witches. If they sank, they were not, and were rescued.

HOW TO MEET A WITCH

First, put your clothes on inside out. Then walk backward to where two roads meet. If you wait until midnight, you will see a witch!

Hex signs on barns are said to keep witches away.

Q. When does a witch know it's time to trick or treat?

A. She looks at her witch-watch.

Q. Why was there no food left after the monster's party?

A. Because everybody was a-goblin.

Q. When do black cats scratch themselves?

A. When they have w-itches.

Male witches were often called warlocks.

"Double, double toil and trouble;
Fire burn, and cauldron bubble."
WILLIAM SHAKESPEARE

WHY ARE CATS AND BATS HALLOWEEN SYMBOLS?

Do you think it is bad luck if a black cat crosses your path? Are you afraid that a bat might suck your blood? If you do, you are not alone, for many people still believe these superstitions about cats and bats.

Long ago, people thought cats and bats had magical powers. Why? Because both move so mysteriously in the dark, without making noise. Cats can see well at night, eyes glowing eerily in the dark. Bats swoop through the nighttime sky as if guided by something unseen.

Cats became part of Halloween because people associated them closely with witches. People thought witches changed into cats to sneak around. They thought cats carried messages between the Devil and witches. Cats were even believed to be mysterious spirits sent to haunt people. Because people feared them, cats were burned during the Samhain festival.

Bats, which frighten people in the dark as they zip in and out of sight, also became Halloween symbols. Some people thought witches could turn themselves into bats in order to get around better.

Perhaps the most famous bat of all is the vampire bat. It is true that vampire bats drink blood, but you do not have to worry. Vampire bats live in Central and South America and prefer the blood of donkeys, pigs, cows, and chickens to that of humans.

Dracula is the best-known blood-sucking human vampire. Dracula was a real man. He was Prince Vlad, a cruel prince of Walachia, now Romania. During his reign he killed many people by driving stakes through their hearts. Dracula, or "son of the Dragon," was his nickname.

Bram Stoker wrote the book *Dracula* based on the evil Prince Vlad and made him famous around the world.

Sunlight is supposed to kill vampires.

If a witch died, her cat would die, too.

Witches sometimes cooked bats in their stews.

Shooting a vampire with a silver bullet is supposed to kill it.

Witches sometimes poured bat blood on themselves before a ceremony.

Wearing garlic around your neck will keep vampires (and everyone else) away!

In many parts of the world, people believe that the souls of dead people became bats.

Some people believed that cat bones made you invisible.

Some witches kept spiders to help them weave their spells.

Q. Where does Dracula go on Halloween?

A. The Vampire State Building.

Q. What is a vampire's least favorite food?

A. A steak.

Q. Where do most cats live?

A. In Connecti-cat.

Q. Where does a witch get a new cat?

A. From a cat-alog.

Q. Why did the witch cry when she lost her cat?

A. It was a cat-astrophe.

Q. Why do witches like butterflies?

A. Because they were once cat-erpillars.

Q. Why do witches like baseball?

A. Because they can hit with a bat and cat-ch with a cat.

WHY DO WE TRICK OR TREAT IN COSTUMES ON HALLOWEEN?

For thousands of years people have dressed up in costumes and masks pretending to be someone or something they weren't. Kings and queens would have special costume parties. Their guests would wear fancy costumes, and everyone would try to guess who was who. One king even dressed up as a living tree to fool his guests! Other people wore costumes when they posed for paintings.

Wearing masks is also an old tradition. Long ago, people wore animal masks to give them power over the animals they hunted. Actors and actresses wore masks instead of makeup in plays. Other people wore scary masks to frighten away demons, which they thought were killing their cattle or stopping the rain from falling.

Witches wore masks or painted their faces black during their Witches' Sabbath. Important people attending the Witches' Sabbath would wear masks so that no one would recognize them. Some people wore masks and costumes to fool evil spirits they thought were looking for them. Farmers and their families would march around their fields wearing masks and carrying torches to keep their fields and animals safe from evil spirits.

When the Irish came to America, they brought many of their traditions with them. One tradition was going from house to house on Halloween to ask for money and food for feasts honoring the dead. If they didn't get a treat, they would play tricks, such as turning over a cart or nailing a gate shut.

Soon children were going from house to house on Halloween to ask for treats. They dressed up in masks and costumes to keep their neighbors from guessing who played tricks on them.

Halloween means trick-or-treating in costumes, Jack-o'-Lanterns, candy, witches on brooms, black cats, bats, and ghosts. Halloween means being a little scared, but knowing we're safe. Most of all, Halloween means fun!

HAPPY HALLOWEEN!

200 years ago people gave buns, pennies, nuts, and apples as treats on Halloween.

Q. What do ghosts wear in the rain?

A. Boo-ts.

Q. Who goes trick-or-treating at the beach on Halloween?

A. Sand-witches.

Q. Why did the baby vampire bat wake up screaming?

A. He had bite-mares.

Q. What animal plays baseball on Halloween?

A. A bat.

Q. What kind of tape do you use on Halloween?

A. Mask-ing tape.

Q. Why can't skeletons go trick-or-treating?

A. They have no-body to go with.

Long ago in England, fireworks were shot off to celebrate Halloween.

PAPER BAG MASKS

Upside-down grocery bags with cutouts for your eyes can be decorated with glitter, yarn, paint, felt markers, colored paper— anything! Either decorate all around or put another face on the back! Cut bag to fit over shoulders. Cut large eyeholes and make sure you can see clearly.

ANIMAL

Paste on ears and whiskers.

ROBOT

Paste on pipe cleaner antennae. Use tinfoil to decorate sides and back.

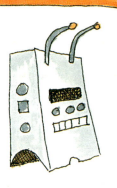

MONSTER

Paint bag green. Paste on cardboard teeth and bones.

DEVIL

Paste red or yellow cellophane over eyeholes. Paste on horns, beard, mustache, and eyebrows.

CLOWN

Use curling ribbon for multicolored hair. Give yourself a funny hat. Paint face or use colored paper.

KING

Make a crown of tinfoil taped to cardboard. Use strips of construction paper or yarn for hair and beard.

PAINTED FACES

Makeup and wigs can make you feel like the person you've dressed up to be. Wigs can be made with old bathing caps, hats, clean mop heads, or old stockings.

DOLL

Make a wig from heavy orange yarn. Use makeup to give yourself a pretty doll face.

CLOWN

Decorate a shower cap with construction-paper or tissue-paper flowers. Paint on big white lips and colored triangles around your eyes.

GHOUL

Powder hair with flour. Paint face white and draw black circles around eyes.

ELEPHANT

Tie off one leg of an old pair of tights and cut off excess. Stuff other leg for nose. Attach felt ears and draw on eyes.

MAKE YOUR OWN COSTUME

WITCH

CONSTRUCTION-PAPER CONE HAT

YARN WIG

PUTTY WARTS AND NOSE

DARK EYESHADOW ON CHEEKS OR PALE-GREEN FACE PAINT

FAKE NAILS PAINTED GRUESOME GREEN OR BLOOD RED!

LONG BLACK SKIRT

BROOM

LARGE BLACK SOCKS OVER SHOES WITH GOLD PAPER BUCKLES PINNED ON

SUPERHERO

TINFOIL HELMET

CARDBOARD SWORD COVERED WITH TINFOIL

SWEATSHIRT STUFFED WITH PADDING

PAPER EMBLEM WITH INITIAL PINNED ON

PLASTIC OR CLOTH CAPE

BOOTS OF CARDBOARD TUBES COVERED WITH TINFOIL

CAT

BLACK HEADBAND WITH PAPER EARS

CUT ONE LEG OFF BLACK TIGHTS AND STUFF OTHER LEG TO MAKE TAIL. DON'T CUT OFF THE WAISTBAND!

BLACK SOCKS WITH PAPER KITTY CLAWS

SAMURAI

HEADBAND
WITH SYMBOL

MAKEUP ON EYES

LONG BATHROBE

COLORFUL SASH

DOUBLE SWORDS
MADE OF CARDBOARD
COVERED WITH TINFOIL

THONG SANDALS
WITH SOCKS

CLOWN

FUNNY HAT

CURLY WIG

BOWTIE MADE FROM
BRIGHT NAPKIN

LARGE COLORFUL SHIRT
WITH BIG CARDBOARD
BUTTONS

SUSPENDERS

OVERSIZED JEANS OR
PANTS ROLLED UP

PATCHES PINNED ON

COLORFUL SOCKS

Safety First

- Be sure you can see clearly out of your mask
- Check your costume for loose ends. You want to be able to move and walk freely
- Light colors are seen better in the dark

PILLOWCASE PERSON

STAPLE STRIP OF HEAVY CARDBOARD INSIDE
CLOSED END OF OLD WHITE PILLOWCASE.

CUT OUT EYEHOLES AND ARMHOLES.
DRAW A FACE USING WIDE-TIPPED FELT MARKERS.

MAKE A HAUNTED HOUSE TREAT BOX

You will need:

empty 1/2-gallon milk carton; brown, black, and yellow construction paper; scissors; stapler; tape; glue; yarn or ribbon.

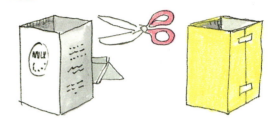

1. Cut off the top of the milk carton. Cover the open carton with yellow paper cut to fit. Tape it in place.

2. Wrap the brown paper, cut to fit, over the yellow and crease the corners. Now draw a front door and several windows. Cut them open. Tape brown paper back in place over the yellow paper.

3. To make a handle, staple braided yarn or ribbon as shown.

4. Open all your doors and windows and draw a Halloween picture inside each. You can draw bats, spiderwebs, witches, Jack-o'-Lanterns. Use your imagination.

5. Cut a black paper roof and glue it to the front of your spooky house.

MAKE CREEPY, CRAWLY SPIDERS

You will need:
black construction paper; black thread or yarn; scissors; stapler; glue or tape; white paint or crayon.

1. Cut a circle out the paper. Make one cut from the outside to the center of the circle. Pull the circle together to form a cone and staple or tape together.

2. Paint or draw two white eyes on the cone, or paste on two white circles.

3. Cut eight long, thin strips of construction paper. Fold in an accordion pleat pattern to form springy legs.

4. Tape, paste, or staple four legs onto the edge of each side of the cone. Let the spider's eyes be your guide.

5. Cut a piece of thread, string, or yarn and poke through the cone top, and knot inside.

HALLOWEEN TREAT RECIPES

SEED SNACK

1. Collect and wash pumpkin and/or acorn squash seeds.

2. Soak the seeds overnight in a bowl of salted water.

3. Drain, and then arrange seeds in a single layer on a lightly oiled cookie sheet.

4. Bake at 250 degrees until seeds are light brown—about an hour. Check occasionally. Stir after 20 minutes.

Enjoy!

CARAMEL APPLES

You will need:

5 apples
1 package of caramels
2 tablespoons hot water
5 Popsicle sticks or clean twigs
double boiler
waxed paper

1. Wash and dry apples and insert stick into stem of each apple.

2. Heat caramels over hot water in double boiler. Stir until smooth.

3. Dip apples into melted caramel, twirling to cover. If you like nuts, roll the bottom of your apple in a dish of crushed peanuts. Place, stick side up, on waxed paper. Refrigerate to harden.

MAKE A HAUNTED HOUSE PARTY

You will need seven bowls to hold:

two rubber gloves filled with wet sand (the hands)
a round sponge soaked in yogurt (the brain)
cooked and cooled spaghetti (the guts)
two wedges of raw potato (the ears)
two peeled grapes (the eyes)
a piece of raw liver (the liver)
candy corn (the teeth)

Make a tape recording of scary sounds—rattle a chain, shake a bag of checkers, and add moans, groans, and screams.

Gather your friends in a dark room. Have them sit in a circle on the floor. Play the tape and, when it is over, push Rewind. Now say, in your scariest voice, "One night I heard a strange sound in my closet (or basement or attic). I went to look and it was a GHOST moaning and groaning and swirling around a pile of stuff on the floor. I ran and got these bowls and scooped up the stuff and the ghost went away. Here's what I found."

Now pass the bowls one at a time while saying, "In this bowl are his HANDS! In this bowl is his BRAIN! In this bowl are his GUTS! In this bowl are his EARS! In this bowl are his EYES! In this bowl is his LIVER! In this bowl is his TEETH!

Then, in your spookiest, scariest voice say, "Oh my gosh, he's come back to get them!" Hit Play, and scream!

Watch your friends jump!

FINGER PLAY SONG/RHYME

"FIVE LITTLE PUMPKINS SITTING ON A GATE"

(Color your fingertips orange. With a black marker make a Jack-o'-Lantern face on each pumpkin finger. Hold up all five fingers.)

Five little pumpkins sitting on a gate,
The first one said,
"Oh my, it's getting late."
The second one said,
"But we don't care."
The third one said,
" I see witches in the air."
The fourth one said,
"Let's run, and run, and run."
The fifth one said,
"Get ready for some fun."
Then whoosh went the wind,
(clap hands)
and out went the lights,
And five little pumpkins rolled
out of sight!
(rolling motion with hands)

BOBBING FOR APPLES

Bobbing for apples is an old Halloween game.

You will need about ten apples and a tub of water. A deep pan or turkey roaster will be great!

Put the apples into the water and let everyone try to catch an apple before it bobs away. No hands allowed! Have a dry towel handy because someone will surely get wet!

Another way to enjoy this game is to hang each apple from a string and let them swing as you try to bite them.

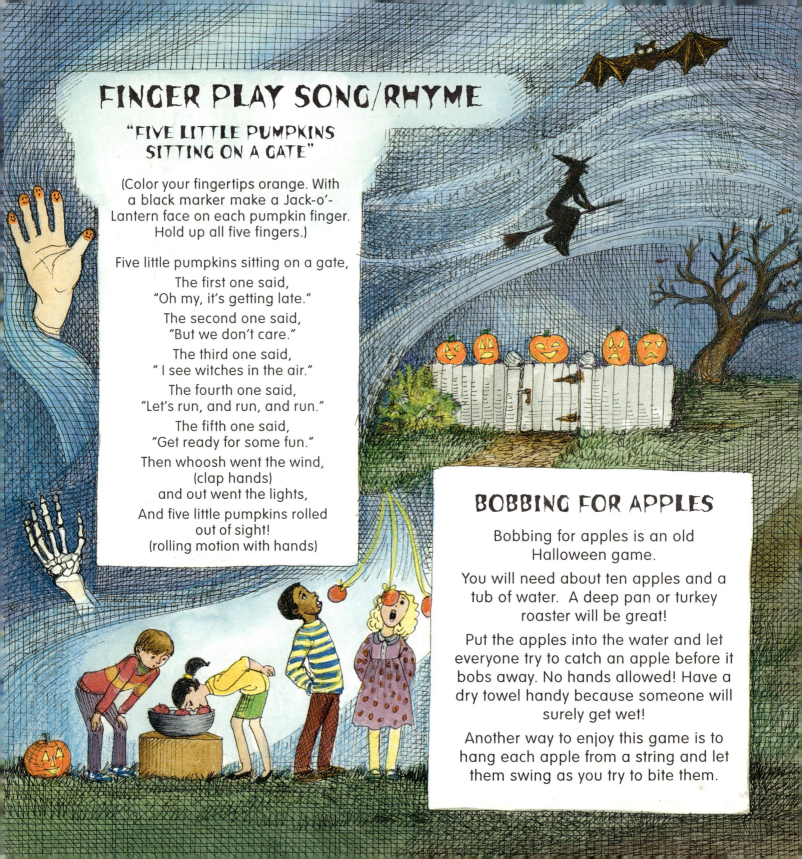

HALLOWE'EN
by Harry Behn

Tonight is the night
When dead leaves fly
Like witches on switches
Across the sky,
When elf and sprite
Flit through the night
On a moony sheen.

Tonight is the night
When leaves make a sound
Like a gnome in his home
Under the ground,
When spooks and trolls
Creep out of holes
Mossy and green.

Tonight is the night
When pumpkins stare
Through sheaves and leaves
Everywhere,
When ghouls and ghost
And goblin host
Dance round their queen.
It's Hallowe'en.

ABOUT THE AUTHORS

Award-winning teachers, Peter and Connie Roop have been tricking and treating their students with Halloween stories for more than twenty years. In their classes the moans and groans you hear are not from ghosts, but from students reacting to their jokes.
With their children, Sterling and Heidi, they have shared many Halloweens trick or treat ing in their neighborhood, eating Halloween treats, and having Halloween parties.

ABOUT THE ARTIST

Katy Keck Arnsteen, artist, writer, teacher, wife, mother, and grandmother has illustrated numerous books for children. She and her friend, a black cat named "Spooky," wish you a HAPPY HALLOWEEN.